ADVANCE YOUR SWAGGER

# ADVANCE YOUR SWAGGER

ADVANCE YOUR SWAGGER

ADVANCE YOUR SWAGGER

ADVANCE YOUR SWAGGER

ADVANCE YOUR SWAGGER

ADVANCE YOUR SWAGGER

ADVANCE YOUR SWAGGER

ADVANCE YOUR SWAGGER

ADVANCE YOUR SWAGGER

FONZWORTH BENTLEY

# ADVANCE YOUR SWAGGER

HOW TO USE

MANNERS,

CONFIDENCE,

AND STYLE

TO GET AHEAD

Ⓥ VILLARD BOOKS | NEW YORK

Published in the United States by Villard Books, an imprint of
The Random House Publishing Group, a division of
Random House, Inc., New York.

VILLARD and "V" CIRCLED Design are registered trademarks
of Random House, Inc.

All photographs courtesy
of the author

Library of Congress Cataloging-in-Publication Data

Bentley, Fonzworth.
Advance your swagger : how to use manners, confidence, and style to
get ahead / by Fonzworth Bentley.
    p.      cm.
ISBN 978-1-4000-6453-3 (hardcover : alk. paper)
1. Etiquette.   I. Title.
BJ1853.B44   2007
395—dc22        2007021093

Printed in the United States of America on acid-free paper

www.villard.com

9 8 7 6 5 4

Book design by Jo Anne Metsch

This book is dedicated to my parents, grandparents, great-grandparents,
aunts, uncles, teachers, coaches, and neighbors who loved
me enough to correct me.
Thank you.
I listened!

Rev. William Debro
"Grandpapa Daddy"

Mary Debro

Rev. Lewis Hooper
"Pipi"

Minnie Hooper
"Mother Dear"

Emmit and Gail
Watkins
"Daddy Emmit and
Mama Gail"

Carrie Hightower
Watson
"Mama Carrie"

Duffie Watson
"Papa Duffie"

Rev. James Debro, Sr.
"Grandad"

Anna Hooper
Debro
"Nana"

Oscar Watkins
"Grandaddy"

Lucy Watson
Watkins
"Grandma"

Harriette Debro
Watkins
"Mom"

My younger brother, Dion Watkins, and me,
Derek Watkins (aka Fonzworth Bentley)

Fred Watkins
"Dad"

# CONTENTS

# PREFACE

How did I, a guy from Atlanta, Georgia, move to New York City without knowing a soul in the entertainment industry and become the personal assistant to one of the biggest moguls in hip-hop history, Sean "Diddy" Combs, in under two years? And then how was I able to transform that opportunity, brand myself, and become one of the players in the industry?

Don't get it twisted; it wasn't easy. But of course, nothing worth having is easy. I understand why they say "If you can make it in New York, you can make it anywhere." This was my first time living outside the South, and I had to grow up fast and figure out how to maneuver even faster.

I can attribute my success to three factors: manners, confidence, and style. I honestly believe we are living in the Golden Age of Disrespect. A time when common courtesies such as speaking to folks, smiling, and saying "please" and "thank you" are perceived as making men look soft and women look vulnerable. We rush past one another and think any sign of kindness will be misconstrued as weakness. Looking "hard" is in.

But that's not me!

Manners were essential in my upbringing. I'm a southerner. In my neck of the woods, you are trained to speak to everyone. I wouldn't dare walk down my street in Atlanta without speaking to my neighbors, or cut past someone without saying "excuse me." Doing these things is like breathing to me. So when I moved to New York, I continued to be myself and use the manners that my parents and ancestors instilled in me. Admittedly, some people looked at me as if I were a visitor from Mars, but most thought it was refreshing. I met a lot of influential people, and a lot of doors were opened simply because I followed the traditions of my youth. My manners were the first ingredient that set me apart from my peers.

Now, I'm a Morehouse Man. Morehouse College is the school of Martin Luther King, Jr.; Samuel L. Jackson; Spike Lee; Maynard Jackson, the first African-American mayor of Atlanta; Michael Lomax, president and CEO of the United Negro College Fund; and my dad, Fred Watkins, just to name a few prestigious graduates. To be a Morehouse Man is synonymous with being confident. There is a saying: "You can tell a Morehouse Man, but you can't tell him much." It is that kind of confidence that embodies the culture at Morehouse College. Students there are taught to be distinguished, self-assured, and proud of their heritage. They are taught to "Find a way or make one." This unwavering self-confidence was the second ingredient that set me apart from my peers.

As for style, well, that has been my thing for a long time. I was never that keen on following the crowd. When everyone was wearing oversize jerseys, pants that were way too big, and tennis shoes (you may call them sneakers), I was wearing a three-piece chocolate-brown-and-tan-pinstriped Purple Label suit, a lavender spread-collar shirt, a foulard tie, chocolate-brown suede cap-toe shoes, and of course, a pocket square. I was wearing suits, but I didn't look Wall Street. I was wearing bold colors, but I didn't look hip-hop. I had my own style that was, in many ways, a blend of the two. My unique style became the third ingredient that set me apart from my peers.

MANNERS + CONFIDENCE + STYLE = SWAGGER. That formula is what this book is all about.

Chances are, you want to know a little something about how to work your swagger. I think you want to know how *you* can break in to whatever business or profession you're striving for so you, too, can live out your dream.

I get that.

You might have picked up this book because you went to a fancy dinner or an upscale restaurant and didn't know which glass was yours or which fork went with which knife. Or there are times when you need to put down the throwback, white tee, and Nike and put on a suit, but you don't know how to tie it together. You're ready to step up your game.

I get that.

I'm going to give you the answers to many of your questions. We'll talk about table manners. We'll talk about how to put together your dress for any occasion. We'll talk about how to land that job you want. And then we'll talk about "brushing your shoulders off." Yes, y'all, we will go there—dealing with haters. Because you know, like I know, that once you get your swagger right, the haters will most definitely show up.

In other words, this book is about you! It's about helping you get to the next level. It's about getting ahead so you can be the man or woman you were meant to be.

I will share with you a few personal stories so you can see what worked and didn't work for me. Throughout the book, you'll see "Bent Hints," which are those little things you should keep in your hip pocket at all times. They are that one bit of 411 to help get you through if you forget everything else.

I hope that after you read this book, you will see that being successful is all about the way you carry yourself, the respect you have for others, and the respect you have for yourself. In other words, it's all those little lessons that your mother or grandmother tried to teach you when you were a "shawty," as we say in the ATL, but either you didn't listen because you didn't think they were that important, or you have simply forgotten and need a refresher.

My parents taught my younger brother and me to "Start where you are, use what you have, and do the very best you can." They told us if we followed these principles, we would be successful no matter what we did in life. These principles worked for me, this guy from Atlanta, Georgia, who moved to New York City without knowing a soul in the entertainment industry and found his dream.

And they can work for you, too.

Now let's get started.

# MANNERS

ADVANCE YOUR SWAGGER

ADVANCE YOUR SWAGGER

THE BROTHER OR SISTER

WHO DOES NOT RESPECT THE

TRADITIONS OF THE ELDERS

WILL NOT BE ALLOWED

TO EAT WITH THE ELDERS.

—AFRICAN PROVERB

ADVANCE YOUR SWAGGER

ADVANCE YOUR SWAGGER

ADVANCE YOUR SWAGGER

ADVANCE YOUR SWAGGER

# CHAPTER 1

# THE MAGIC OF "PLEASE" AND "THANK YOU"

I am beginning this book with manners. Hold on. Don't turn the page yet. You see, I believe your swagger comes from the inside out. It doesn't matter how good you look, how stylish you are, or how confident you appear. If you are rude, crude, or unpolished, you will not get very far in any game and stay there. After all, who wants to be around anyone who doesn't respect others or him- or herself?

I think one of the most important lessons I have learned in life is about relationships. You can go just about anywhere and do just about anything if people know you, like you, and feel comfortable with you. I believe knowing how to treat people well is a very important ingredient for success, no matter what profession you choose.

And it all begins with three little words, "please" and "thank you."

My parents were sticklers for making my brother and me use what they called "the magic words": "please" and "thank you." If we didn't say "please," we didn't get anything. If we didn't say "thank you," what we got was taken back. When you're a kid, you learn pretty quickly how to get what you want. So if saying "please" and "thank you" got me what I wanted, then "please" and "thank you" were the way to go. After all, it didn't take much sweat to say them, and it reaped fantastic results.

It worked when I met Sean "Diddy" Combs.

I had met Diddy on several occasions when I was working retail in Atlanta and in and around clubs after I moved to New York. Whenever I ran into him, he always complimented me on the way I dressed. One night at a club, he told me he liked the way I put my threads together and asked me to work on his wardrobe. He gave me his two-way number information. I tried several times to reach out to him but never received a callback. Having worked for Diddy, I now know why he didn't return my calls initially. This man is extremely busy and stays on the phone. Everyone in the world tries to get ahold of him.

Well, one day I was having a really bad time on my job. I was maître d' at one of New York City's finest restaurants. I loved my job, but it had reached a point when I knew it was time for me to make my move. After all, I hadn't moved to New York from Atlanta to have a career in the hospitality business. My sole purpose for moving to the Big Apple was to break in to entertainment. I had to get my eyes back on the prize.

On this day, I decided to go for it. I texted Diddy with a message that read something like this: "Do you remember when you left Howard University to intern with Andre Harrell so that you could follow your dream? Well, I'm that guy in 2001. **PLEASE** give me an opportunity to follow my dream." Diddy hit me back: "If you can be at this address in ten minutes, we'll talk." I was two blocks away and ran all the way there.

The location he gave me was a restaurant, and when I walked in, I was excited and exhausted, with my adrenaline on overdrive. Diddy's executive assistant and one of his homies were there. I sat down and immediately started talking about myself and why I needed to work for him. I was talking a mile a minute.

Needless to say, no one was impressed with me. I remember his

I'm teaching my cousin, Grace, the magic of "please" and "thank you," and she's not too happy about it. But if she wants this orange . . .

All right, now she gets it!

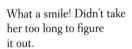

What a smile! Didn't take her too long to figure it out.

homeboy said, "Man, you talk too much." Diddy's executive assistant agreed. She said I did too much talking and not enough listening. Diddy told me I couldn't have the job, to leave, and to have a nice life.

That was when another one of my childhood teachings kicked in. I slowed down, turned to his homeboy, and looked him straight in the eyes as he was telling me all the things I was doing wrong. Then, in the middle of his sentence, he stopped and said, "But I like the way you look people in the eyes."

I turned to Diddy and looked him straight in the eyes and said, "I'm not going to take no for an answer. *Please* give me an opportunity." That was when the tables turned.

Now, was "please" the magic word that got me the job? I don't know, but you'd better believe I didn't want to take any chances. I used the word. I looked him straight in the eyes. I got the job!

Think about it—when was the last time you said "please" or "thank you" to anyone? Many of your homies might think you've gone soft, but take another look at them. Do they really have what you want in life? You've tried it their way: being tough, ungrateful, expecting the world to owe you something. In the words of Dr. Phil, "Is that working for you?" If not, I challenge you to try this approach for just one month. I promise you, you will see a drastic change in your attitude and therefore in your life.

BENT HINT: "Please" and "thank you" are words that can carry you a long way in this world. They are empowering words that can help open many doors. When you are grateful, the universe has a way of honoring you and assisting you on your journey through life. They are small words with powerful impact.

# CHAPTER 2

# HEY, THAT'S MY FORK

When I was in college, I was invited to have dinner at the home of a very famous man in the entertainment business. I was extremely honored and starstruck over the fact that I'd been invited to this most amazing home with this most amazing man and his family.

We were served a delicious meal, and I ate with my "best home training" manners. At the end of the meal, my host said to me, "Son, I like the way you handle your knife and fork." Wow, he'd been paying attention to the way I was eating. I had no idea he was watching me. By the way, that famous entertainer was Bill Cosby, who has been a very positive influence in my career.

Folks really do observe how we eat, how we handle our fork and knife, and how we behave at the table. Manners really do matter.

I'm in restaurants all the time, and as I told you earlier, I used to work in one of the best ones in New York. I have seen it all. I used to get pretty annoyed with some of the terrible table manners I saw. Then it hit me! Most of the folks in my generation and those younger than mine had grown up eating from white paper bags. You know, the fast-food stuff. We're used to eating with our fingers. It's fun eating. We grab our sacks and we continue to eat while we're doing everything else in the world, such as driving, talking on the phone, laughing, or clowning around. Eating is not an *experience* for my generation; it's something we have to do. That's why we don't take the time to learn or even notice the "proper" way to eat. Then, when we are at a special event or in an upscale restaurant, we don't know what to do. But we're growing up now. We will be put in situations where we need to know what to do and what not to do.

Here are the basics.

## TABLE SETTING

Don't be intimidated by this more formal place setting. Remember that things you eat from are to the left of your plate (such as your bread plate) and things you drink from are to the right of your plate (in this case, a water glass and red wineglass). As for the utensils, you will generally work from the outside in as the courses progress. To the left of your plate: salad fork, dinner fork. In the center: plate and soup bowl. To the right of your plate: dinner knife, salad knife, teaspoon, soup spoon. Above the plate: dessert fork and spoon. And if you can't remember, you can always follow someone else's lead at the table.

## WHICH GLASS IS MINE?

I practice this guideline: Everything you drink is to the right of your plate. Things you eat, like your bread, are to the left of your plate.

This is a casual place setting. To the left of the plate: salad fork, dinner fork. To the right of the plate: dinner knife and teaspoon. Note that the glass should be at the tip of your knife.

## WHEN DO YOU BEGIN EATING?

If it's a sit-down meal, *wait* until everyone at your table has been served before you begin eating. Let me say it again. **Wait** until *everyone* at your table has been served before you begin eating. Come on, folks, the food ain't goin' nowhere, and you can wait a second or two.

If the dinner is a buffet, it's okay to begin eating when you sit down; however, I'm more comfortable waiting until at least one other person sits at my table before I begin eating.

He's eating without me! Oh, no, he didn't. And he threw his tie over his shoulder? One more strike, and he's out!

## USING THE KNIFE AND FORK

Please don't stab your food! This is all wrong.

Check out how I'm holding my knife and fork. Practice, practice, practice.

Please get this right or you'll tell on yourself.

## EATING BREAD

How do you eat bread? One bite at a time. I see this mistake all the time, and I must admit, I flub it every once in a while.

Take your bread, break off one bite-size chunk, butter it if you choose,

11

and eat it. Please do not butter the entire piece of bread at one time. And please, please don't pick up the entire piece of bread and eat from it. Not a good look. The only exception to this is if you're eating some good hot biscuits. You have to butter the whole thing while it's hot. There's nothing better.

Don't butter the whole roll—take your time!

See how silly it looks to eat from the whole roll?

Break off a piece of
your roll and butter it.

Eat one piece
at a time.

## TALKING AND EATING

Can't be done, shouldn't be done, please don't do it!

There's nothing worse than eating a meal with a friend who is telling you a story while he's eating. The next thing you know, the food that he's eating lands on your plate. It pisses you off, and it embarrasses your friend. So don't do it. The best part about eating with a friend is that you both will have time to eat and talk. Just don't do it at the same time. Plus, who wants to look into someone's mouth when he's chewing his food? Not a good look. Wait. I will say it again—wait. You will have plenty of time to talk and plenty of time to eat.

## CAN I PUT MY ELBOW ON THE TABLE?

Yes and no. Yes, before your meal is served, it's okay to have a little elbow on the table while you're talking and waiting for your food to be served. Once your plate is put before you, the elbows must get off the table and stay off while you're eating. Once you've completed your meal and your place setting has been removed, it's okay to get in a relaxed and casual position and put your elbows back on the table.

Once your plate is removed, you can put your elbows on the table.

## HOW DO YOU PASS FOOD?

Most guidelines will say pass to your right. I have to admit, I really don't care if you pass to the right or left, just pass the food while it's still in the serving dish.

Not long ago, I was having dinner with several of my friends. I asked my homeboy, who was seated closest to the breadbasket, to pass me the bread. This nut picked up a piece of bread out of the basket and handed it to me. I mean, come on! He didn't mean any harm. He just didn't know any better. Now you know. Don't put your hands on someone else's food. You know you wrong!

## HOW TO HANDLE THE NAPKIN?

Place the napkin on your lap in a half-folded position. Use your napkin a lot to make sure you remove that nasty little piece of food that's hanging at the edge of your lips. Remember, most folks are shady and won't tell you when you have that piece of lettuce in the corner of your mouth. All of a sudden they will stop looking at you because you look nasty. So you have to be mindful and use that napkin.

If you get up from the table for a short period of time, place your napkin either on the back

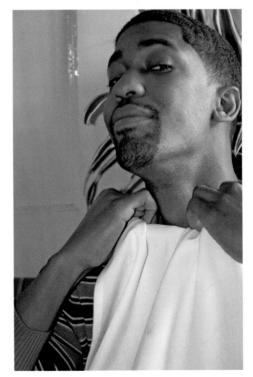

You need a bib only if you're eating lobster or you're a baby. Put that napkin down!

15

of your chair or on the arm of your chair. It's best not to put a dirty napkin on the table while others are still eating and you're away. When you complete your meal, you may then put your napkin on the table or in your plate.

Now fold your napkin in half and place it in your lap.

By placing my fork and knife near the bottom of my plate, I am letting the waiter know that I am still eating but am taking a break.

Close out position. By placing my fork and knife in the 3:15 position, I am letting the waiter know that I am finished with my meal and it is okay to remove my plate.

## CAN I USE A TOOTHPICK AFTER THE MEAL?

Yes, as soon as you get in your car. Please don't walk out of the restaurant with a toothpick in your mouth. It's not important to anybody that you've got food stuck in your mouth. Leave the toothpick until you are in a private place or private plane.

Bentley, please.
Take that toothpick
out of your mouth.

You know you
wrong for that!

BENT HINT: If all else fails, keep your antennae up. Observe your host and follow his or her lead. It's amazing how much you can learn by taking the time to look up and see how other folks are doing their thing—not just with eating but in other social situations as well.

# CHAPTER 3

# FINE DINING

When I began working for Diddy, my mother called me and said, "Please don't lose that man's stuff." She knew me too well. She knew that my biggest weaknesses were organization and keeping track of things. But I knew I would shine in the fine-dining arena.

Everyone knows most personal assistants do not sit at the dinner table while their boss is engaged in important meetings. Most P.A.s will sit in the car or stay outside to catch up on their calls, etc. But I wanted to learn and hear how deals were made and see firsthand how negotiations were done. However, I needed an excuse to stay in the room. So, being the hustler that I am, I "captained" the station and had the restaurant server assist me as I led the service for the table.

It paid off.

I was able to get an MBA at Sean Combs College, which is highly accredited. And in the process, I met the likes of the designer Donatella Versace and Thomas Freston, chairman and CEO of MTV Networks, to name just two.

That's why it's important to learn how to feel comfortable and know your way around in a fine-dining environment. You never know who you will meet and what you will learn.

Here are some tips.

## RESERVATIONS

Your fine-dining experience begins with the reservation. Please don't walk into an upscale restaurant at seven-thirty P.M., knowing you haven't made a reservation, and expect to get a table. It ain't gonna happen. If the restaurant is very popular, you should make your reservations at least a week or two in advance.

When you call to make your reservations, here are some things you need to share with the host:

- Your name
- How many people are in your party
- The date and time you desire
- If this is a special occasion (birthday, anniversary, etc.)
- Any dietary concerns
- Special table request (near a window, private area, nonsmoking, etc.)

You should ask the host:

- What credit cards are accepted
- Dress code (do men need a jacket, etc.)
- Parking instructions

## WHEN YOU ARRIVE

If you arrive at the restaurant before your guests, give the maître d' your name and let him or her know you have a reservation and you are waiting for your other guests to arrive. Most restaurants will not seat you until your entire party arrives. Now is a good time to introduce yourself to the bar. If you're the legal age, of course.

## COAT CHECK

A gentleman should check his hat, coat, and umbrella as well as those of his guests. The host will give you a ticket that will be used to identify your belongings. Be sure to hang on to this ticket. At the end of your dinner, give the host your ticket, get your belongings, and leave a tip (more about that in Chapter 4).

## SEATING

When you and your guests are seated, your server will come to your table, introduce him- or herself, and welcome you. This is your time to set yourself apart. Remember, the server is a real person, so when she gives you her name, use it. Tell her you are delighted to be a guest at the restaurant because you've heard nothing but wonderful things about it. This helps to set the tone and your expectations for a great evening.

If you were waiting at the bar before you were seated, it's okay to bring your drink to the table with you. You can either close out your bill at the bar or ask that the drinks be added to your dinner bill.

Your server will ask for your drink order first. Be prepared to answer. When you receive the menu, you and your guests should take the time to look it over and ask any questions you might have, either about how a dish is prepared or about the specials. Don't be shy. If you want to know, ask.

BENT HINT: The best way to let your waiter know you are ready to order is to close your menu and put it to the side of your table. If you don't know what you want to order, ask your server for a recommendation. Servers love to assist. That's part of their job, and they take a lot of pride in helping their guests. Use their knowledge, and you can't go wrong . . . most of the time.

## WHAT TO ORDER?

When you are the guest, don't order the most expensive thing on the menu. That's rude. Take your lead from your host. Ask your host, "What would you recommend?" or "What are you having?" The answer will give you an idea of the appropriate price range for your order.

I like to leave it up to my host to order an appetizer. Usually, the host will order appetizers for the table. If your host doesn't order an appetizer, then you shouldn't, either.

The host will also take the lead for ordering wine. Ordering wine could be another book entirely, so I won't go into all of those details. The main deal I want you to take away about wine is to ask your waiter for a recommendation, or to ask the sommelier (a wine steward who knows the restaurant's wines and what food they're best paired with). Don't be intimidated by wine. If you like a wine, it's the best one for your meal. If you don't like it, send it back. Keep in mind, just because you don't necessarily like the **taste** of the wine doesn't mean you can send it back without paying for it. However, if the sommelier suggested the wine and you don't like it, you can send it back without having to pay. Or, if the wine tastes like vinegar or it's corked, send it back and you shouldn't have to pay. Most restaurants are more understanding if you send back a glass of wine that doesn't work for you than a bottle of wine. That's why I like to stick close to the sommelier. That's what they get paid to do.

## WHO SHOULD PAY?

If you invite someone for a meal, you should expect to pay unless you made it clear up front that this is dutch treat, meaning each person pays his or her own way.

Okay, I'm ballin' this time. I'll pick up the check.

Um, Faune, can you help a brother out?

Once I had an acquaintance invite me to dinner to discuss a business idea he wanted to run by me. He chose a very expensive restaurant, but when the check came, he didn't make a move to pick it up. It didn't take me too long to realize he wasn't going to pay. I picked up the check, but you'd better believe that was the last meal this guy will ever get from me.

I'm an old-fashioned guy, so I always pay for my girl. There are times, however, when she likes to treat me, and I never refuse that offer. Ladies, take a hint: Men love to be treated every once in a while. Ladies, take a hint: Men love to be treated every once in a while. Ladies, take a hint: Men love to be treated every once in a while. A Mike J-O-N-E-S three-some!

BENT HINT: When you arrive, you can discreetly tell the waiter or maître d' to give you the check to avoid an argument over who's going to pay.

## OTHER HINTS FOR A WONDERFUL MEAL

- If you drop your napkin or silverware, don't pick it up. Use your foot and push it under the table, then ask the waiter to please give you another one.
- If you put something in your mouth and you don't like the taste, discreetly remove it with your fork and place it to the side of your plate. I like to hide it under the parsley; after all, who eats parsley?
- Remember to cut your food one bite at a time. Don't cut up all your food at one time, like your mother used to do for you when you were a kid.

Did your mama cut up your food for you? Remember, you should cut only one bite at a time.

- Don't broadcast the cost of the meal. No one wants to know if you're ballin' or on a budget. Keep it private.
- If you are the guest, please don't complain about the food, the lighting, the service, or the restaurant. Remember, you are a guest, and you should only show appreciation. There's nothing worse than a complainer.
- If you order something and it's not cooked to your liking, just quietly and politely tell the waiter what the issue is; he will do everything to take care of you. Example: You order steak and ask for medium well, but when it arrives, it's rare. Don't make a big deal out of it, just quietly tell your waiter.
- If you find hair in your food, don't yell about it at the top of your voice. In this case, I wouldn't even let my host know. You can simply call the waiter over and quietly show him the hair. The waiter will immediately remove your plate and bring you another.

- If you spill something, don't jump and holler, "Oh, look what I did!" Quietly apologize and ask for the waiter. You're eating; spills will happen.
- Ladies, please don't refresh your makeup at the table. You are not auditioning for *America's Next Top Model*. Excuse yourself and go to the ladies' room.
- Purses and briefcases belong on the floor or an empty seat, not on the table.
- No double-dipping. If there's dip or a sauce for the table, don't use the chip or cracker that you're eating to go back to the dish for more.
- Remember, the salt and pepper shakers are married to each other. When passing, pass both at the same time. Speaking of salt, don't add any before you taste your food.
- Don't blow on your soup if it's too hot. Let it cool, then dip your spoon in the bowl; let it cool, then put it in your mouth.

Hey, don't be leaning all into your soup.

Stop that blowing, or your soup will fly everywhere.

There you go, sit up straight.

Make sure you spoon the soup away from you.

Hold it there, now lap it up. Umm-umm, good!

- Pay attention to your host. Try not to finish your meal much faster than everyone else at the table. Slow it down.
- When the meal is over, be sure to thank your host. Don't just get up and leave. Remember, "thank you" is magical.
- The key words for a lovely meal are:

  Be discreet

  Be observant

  Be nice

  Be thankful

BENT HINT: I make it a point to be especially nice to people who are handling my food. My motto is: "Don't mess with anyone who is messing with my food." Do you feel me? If you want good service, being nice goes a long way.

# CHAPTER 4

# DON'T TIP OUT

Ah, let's deal with tipping. Most people either don't want to tip, don't know how much to tip, or don't know it's important to tip. Because I spent three years working in the hospitality business, I am hypersensitive to the importance of tipping. People who work in the service industry work very hard for their money, and many depend on tips to make ends meet. I am also aware that there are a few who might slack off every once in a while, but basically, most do an excellent job day in and day out.

A tip is a way of giving a token of appreciation to those who have helped to lighten your load, to create a delightful dining experience, or to make you look good. A tip lets them know you value their service.

Tipping can be a little confusing, but here are some general guidelines that I use.

## RESTAURANT

I know you should tip on the bill before tax, but I usually tip on the total bill, including tax. I think working in the restaurant business made me more appreciative and understanding of the work these ladies and gentlemen do.

Informal dining—15–20 percent

Fine dining—20–25 percent

Coat check—$1 per item, but if it's a fur, you might want to add a little more to ensure you get it back . . . HOLLA!

Many restaurants will charge an 18–20 percent gratuity on parties of six or more people.

BENT HINT: The best way to figure out the tip is to get a tip card. Depending on the state tax, you can double the tax and add $1 or $2.

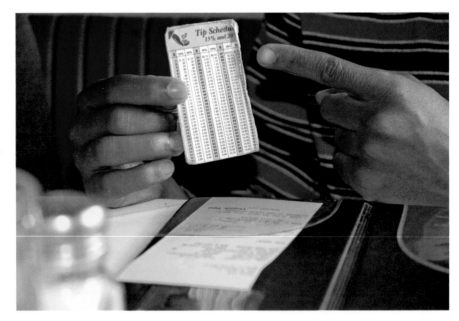

As you can see, I use my tip card a lot!

Here are some other tipping guidelines.

## AIRPORT

Skycap—$2 a bag

## BARBERSHOP

Barber—15–20 percent of total bill
Shampooer—$2

## BEAUTY SHOP

Stylist—15–20 percent of total bill
Shampooer—$2–$5

## SPA SALON

Manicurist—$2–$5
Pedicurist—$5 or 15 percent of total bill
Combined service—15 percent

## VALET PARKING

$2 (tip when the car is brought back to you)

## HOTEL

Housekeeping—$2–$5 per night at end of stay
Bellman—$2 per bag or $10 for carrying luggage to the room

Room service—be sure to read the fine print on your bill, because many hotels include the room-service tip in the bill. If it's not included, 20 percent is a good guide.

## TAXI

15 percent or more of total bill if driver helps with luggage

**By all means, if or when you reach baller status, forget these guidelines and really take care of your folks!**

# CHAPTER 5

# YOUR ANYTIME MINUTES ARE NOT FOR ANYTIME

The cell phone is one of the greatest and most widely used necessities since the invention of fire. My grandparents could not have dreamed that one day you'd be able to walk around anywhere in the world and receive a call in your hip pocket. For them, it was a miracle when they received a call in their home. But now you ought to see my grandmother ballin' with the earpiece.

With this great innovation, there is a need for major consideration. Because the phone has gone beyond the privacy of the home, we have to be even more mindful of our surroundings and the impact our phones can be having on others. I think you know where I'm going with this.

The phone's primary purpose is to provide a convenient conversation between two people: the caller and the receiver. Don't nobody else want to hear that your lil' cousin can't pay his car note. Keep it private.

One day I was in the coffee shop and overheard someone on a cell phone talking about a friend of mine. Now, I'm no snitch. I didn't tell my friend that someone was talking bad about him behind his back, but I will tell you that whenever I see that guy, I always look at him with a squinted eye.

I know she's not going to answer that call.

She's talking overtime and enjoying it!

Okay, we both can play that game!

## "RING" THE ALARM

Isn't it interesting how annoying it is to hear a phone ringing in a public place? That is, of course, until you realize it's your phone that's ringing. Trust me, when the cell phone goes off in public, it's a pain in the butt for everyone.

When you are in a public space, please turn off the ringer or put your phone on vibrate. It takes only a second. Think about it. What message are you sending to the person you're with when you answer the phone while he or she is standing there? The message is "This little thing in my hand is more important than you." Remember the song "Love the One You're With"? That is so true when it comes to dealing with the cell phone. It's best to give the person you're with your undivided attention, instead of a voice coming over the phone. Needless to say, if it's an emergency or a very important call you're expecting, then by all means, answer the phone. Just give the person you're with the courtesy of letting her know what's going on. Step off to the side and have your personal conversation with the caller.

I have been to movies, weddings, hospitals, and even funerals and heard someone's phone go off. That's way over the top of rudeness.

Watch out for the ring tones, too!

I had a friend hang out with me one day because he wanted to learn more about the entertainment industry. I invited him to go to a meeting with me so he could experience firsthand what I go through in a day. We were in the middle of this very important meeting when my friend's phone went off. His ring tone said, "PICK UP THE DAMN PHONE!" How embarrassing was that! I'm sure when my friend chose that ring tone, he thought it was funny and kinda hip. It sure wasn't funny or cool that day. You know the rest of the story: That was his first and last time going any place with me.

Now, if you have one of my songs on your ring tone, be as rude as you want . . . otherwise, have some sense when you choose your ring tone.

## CALL WAITING CAN MAKE YOUR DAY OR RUIN SOMEONE ELSE'S

Please don't call and ask my dad to hold on while you click over to another call. I promise you, he will hang up. My generation understands and loves call waiting, but most people over forty can't stand it. Be careful of whom you ask to hold on so you can answer another call. You might get your feelings hurt.

But you know, I don't care how old or young a person is, you shouldn't put anyone on hold for longer than ten seconds. I think making someone hold longer than that puts you in the rude zone. Don't go there.

If you are talking on the phone and another call comes in, you can ignore it, and it will go into voice mail. If it's important, he will call back. If you look at your caller ID and see it's from someone you are expecting, or it could be an emergency, let the caller you're talking to know you need to grab the other line and you will call him right back. Let him tell you he doesn't mind holding or he doesn't mind if you call him back.

If someone has told you she needs to grab the other line, don't ask, "Who's that on the other line?" It ain't your business.

## DON'T LEAVE ME HANGING

All calls should be returned within twenty-four hours. But I know some folks reading this are still waiting for me to call them back . . . my bad!

## I CAN HEAR YOU

As I have said before, your phone conversation should be private. I think it's okay to talk on the phone while walking down the street, but keep your voice low. Cell phones are so advanced that you really don't have to talk loud to be heard on the other end.

Places where I think it's okay and not okay to talk on your cell:

| PLACE | OKAY | NOT OKAY |
|---|---|---|
| Church | | X |
| Movie theater | | X |
| Restaurants | | |
|   ■ Fast food | X *(keep it low)* | |
|   ■ Casual dining | X *(keep it very low)* | |
|   ■ Fine dining | | X |

| Place | Okay | Not Okay |
|---|---|---|
| The mall | x *(keep it low)* | |
| On a date *(unless it ain't going well)* | | x |
| In a store | x *(keep it low)* | |
| In the bank line | | x |
| On a bus | x *(keep it low and short)* | |
| On a train | x *(keep it low and short)* | |
| On a plane *(unless the flight attendant says it's ok)* | | x |
| Doctor's office | | x |
| Spa | | x |
| Club | | x |
| School | | x |
| Elevator | | x |

When you're talking on the phone, it's rude to chew gum or eat in someone's ear. You can hear that on the other end, and it's very annoying. Coughing into the phone is a definite no.

BENT HINT: The key to great cell phone manners is having and showing good judgment. When you are in a public place, remember, your call should be private. Keep it that way. Keep your conversations low and short. It shows you respect others, and just as important, it shows you respect yourself.

# CHAPTER 6

# HIT ME BACK!

For my generation, writing is going to be done in an e-mail or by text messaging. I can't tell you the last time I handwrote a letter. Oh, yes, I can. The last time I wrote a handwritten letter was when I was at summer camp and we had to send a letter home to our parents. I didn't like doing it then, and I sure don't like doing it now.

## THIS IS HOW WE DO IT

First of all, there's a completely different language that we use on our PDA (BlackBerry, Treo, Sidekick, etc.—anybody else who wants a mention, send me a check . . . HOLLA!) than we use in an e-mail on our computer. So let's start with e-mail:

- Don't send an e-mail in all caps. I hate when I get an e-mail like that. It feels like the person is yelling at me. I don't need that.

See how this feels:

WHY DIDN'T YOU PICK ME UP FROM MY HOUSE WHEN
YOU SAID YOU WERE GOING TO?

I NEED TO KNOW ASAP IF YOU WANT TO GO WITH ME.

See what I mean?

- Don't send an e-mail when you're mad or upset. It will probably come back to haunt you, and it's guaranteed to be seen by others. Take a deep breath and, if at all possible, go see the person. If that's not possible, pick up the phone. You can get more issues solved over the phone than in an e-mail battle. I know too many friends who have broken up because of a never-winning e-mail battle.
- Speaking of e-mail battles, if someone sends you a heated message, don't respond to it with another e-mail. Pick up the phone, call the person, and talk it through. You'll get more done that way and maybe save a friendship.
- Be careful before you hit that "send" button. I think faster than I type. That means sometimes all the things I have in my head don't make it to the screen. I'll think I've typed what I have in my mind, but when I reread it, it doesn't always come out that way. When I look back at some of my old e-mails, I sound like an idiot. Take the time to check before you send.
- Use spell-check and grammar-check. Your friends and family might forgive you for all those misspelled words, but your business partners might not.
- Respond to your e-mails within twenty-four hours. If your e-mail program has an office-assistant or "out-of-office" feature, then use it if you are unable to respond within a day's time. Your OA can ex-

plain that you will be away and won't respond to your messages until the date you return.

## NOW FOR THE PERSONAL DIGITAL ASSISTANT (PDA)

I love my PDA. It's so easy to get totally involved with that little device and forget about the people you're with. The PDA can be addictive. I can hardly wait to read a message, and I can hardly wait to respond. But you know what, I can wait. Just like it's rude to talk on the cell when you're with someone, it's rude to text or read a text when you are with someone. Put the thing down. It can wait. Take it out when you're waiting in line at the grocery store, when you're waiting to be served at a restaurant, or when you go to the bathroom. The person you're with deserves more than seeing the top of your head.

Another thing about this little technological wonder—the lights! The lights on these things are really bright, so don't open them up when you're in the movie theater. I was in the movies, and several people opened up their PDAs. It felt like a strobe light was going off. It was extremely annoying.

The key to the PDA, as with the cell phone, is showing respect. If you have to check your messages, say, "Excuse me. I need to check something very quickly, but I'll be off in a second." That's good manners.

# CHAPTER 7

# I SMELL FISH!

After I'd worked for Diddy for a year and a half, I knew it was time for me to move on. I was unsure what route I wanted to take—music, which was my first love, TV, movies—but my eyes were still on the prize of getting into the entertainment business.

When I'd packed my bags and moved from New York to Los Angeles, all I had were a few dollars and a dream. Andre Harrell, Diddy's mentor, let me camp out on his couch. After he got tired of seeing me sleeping on his couch every morning, I found another place to crash: Macy Gray's house.

Macy had an extra bedroom that she said I could stay in for a couple of weeks. I never make up my bed at home, but I've been taught that when you're a guest in someone else's home, you always make up your bed and pitch in on any other house chores. And that's exactly what I did. My couple of weeks turned into three months. I really became a part of the family, and honestly, I believe they were sad to see me go. (Y'all didn't throw a party, did you, Macy?)

When you see me making up a bed, you know I must be a guest!

There are some basic guidelines to follow when you're a guest in someone's home. The main thing to remember is you're not at home!

Have a clear understanding before you arrive of how long you will stay.

Make arrangements for your transportation. Don't expect your host to chauffeur you around unless you have that understanding up front.

Assist with the housework. Make up your bed every day.

Hang up your towels in the bathroom.

When you eat, put your dishes in the sink and volunteer to wash them. (I have to admit, I usually hold my breath in hopes that they'll say, "No, go sit down.") But your host will appreciate the offer.

Treat your host to a nice dinner out as a thank-you for letting you stay.

Bring or buy a nice host gift before you leave—bath salts, a coffee-table book—or mail it with a thank-you note after you get home.

## GUESS WHO'S COMING TO DINNER?

A few years ago, I escorted Naomi Campbell to the NAACP Image Awards. Afterward, Naomi hosted a get-together in her Beverly Hills Hotel suite. It was a star-studded event. We were informed that there was another star trying to get in, but the guy had six of his homies with him. Naomi asked me to please go out and tell him he couldn't get in with his entourage. I felt horrible, but I did it. This star might not have too much of a problem getting in now because he has an Oscar and a Grammy.

BENT HINT: If you're invited for a meal or a party, don't bring others. You were invited, not your cousins, your homies, or your children. Your host knows you have children and friends; if he wants them to come, he'll invite them. Please don't ask if you can bring them. There may be one slight exception: If you have houseguests visiting from out of town, you can inform the people inviting you that you would love to attend but you have out-of-town guests. Leave it up to your host to invite them. I know it's hard, but please don't ask to bring them.

Bring a small token of thanks. A bottle of wine, flowers, candles, or a coffee-table book is always appreciated. I don't like to take candy because so many people are watching their weight.

Show up on time. Don't show up for a dinner thirty minutes or more late. It's very difficult to keep a meal hot. Likewise, don't show up thirty minutes or more early. Your hosts are probably not ready for you, and you will get in the way.

Remember to thank your hosts for a lovely time. If it's a large party, try to find your hosts before you leave to personally thank them. If they are busy with other guests, don't interrupt, but remember to call in the next day or two to express your appreciation.

BENT HINT: Keep in mind that both fish and houseguests stink after three days. In other words, don't stay too long.

## SOCIAL EVENTS

When you receive an invitation, look for the RSVP instructions. RSVP is French for *répondez s'il vous plaît* or, in plain ole English, "please respond." These instructions are the only way the host will know how many people to prepare for. The RSVP will tell you who and where to call and by what date. Be sure to honor this request. I know a lot of y'all will ignore this and just show up. Don't do that! If you didn't say you are coming, then no one is expecting you, and there is no seat for you. It's as simple as that. Take the time to respond.

Keep in mind, only the people on the invitation should respond. If the invitation is addressed to Mr. and Mrs. Fred Watkins, then the response should include only Mr. and Mrs. Fred Watkins. Please don't respond that Mr. and Mrs. Fred Watkins and two children will attend. Got it?

For some large functions, the invitations might say "Regrets only." That means respond only if you are not able to attend. Otherwise, the hosts will assume you are coming.

A thank-you note written to the host is always a gracious thing to do after you've attended a special affair.

If you didn't have a chance to bring a hostess gift with you, then send one in the mail a few days after the event. That's always a nice and welcome surprise.

# CHAPTER 8

# YOU WRONG FOR THAT! (BUT YOU DON'T HAVE TO BE)

There are some things that I can't believe people do, and when I see them, I just want to say, "You wrong for that!" These are the little things that bug not only me but others when they see you do it. They might not tell you, but they see you, and they are pissed.

## PROFANITY

Let's go there. Cursing is definitely overrated. When you think about it, in most cases, it's unnecessary. I will admit, when I stub my toe, there's only one word that can capture the feeling—you know. And there are times when you might decide that a few choice four-letters are perfect for expressing how you feel, but those instances should be few and far between and rarely, if ever, in public.

Early on in my career, I was interviewed by a magazine and got a little too comfortable. I found myself cursing just because I could. Well, my grandmother Nana read that article and called me out on it. That was the end of that!

I spied this young lady walking around the mall as she ate her food. Sis, please hurry up and find the food court.

## MALL MANNERS

Don't go in a store or walk in the mall with your fries, hamburger, and drink. That's why they have a food court.

Don't run in the mall. There are all kinds of people in the mall, young and old. You can hurt someone if you're running. I don't want my ninety-year-old grandmother to get hurt, and I know you don't want anyone to hurt yours, either.

Talking loud is so unnecessary. We see you. We don't need to hear you, too. Turn it down.

## PUBLIC TRANSPORTATION

Our elders are our royalty. If you are sitting and an older person gets on the bus or train, get up and offer him or her your seat. It will make you feel fantastic. And the same goes for pregnant women—wouldn't you have wanted someone to do the same for your mama when she was pregnant with you?

Talking loud is so unnecessary. Turn it down.

## MOVIE MANNERS

No talking or whispering, please. Everyone wants to hear the movie, not you.

Remove your hat. It's hard to see over your head.

Don't put your foot on the back of someone's seat. That's very annoying.

Cut your phone off or put it on vibrate. No one wants to hear your ring or ring tone when the movie is on.

Remember, the lights on your phone and/or PDA can be a major distraction in a dark movie theater. The strobe light is for the club.

You wrong for putting that gum under your chair in the movie. Save the wrapper to put it in, or find a small piece of paper to wrap it in and throw it away.

## AIRPLANE MANNERS

My friend Janet was checking in at the airport, and the attendant told her that her luggage was oversize. She apologized, told the attendant her luggage was new and she hadn't realized the problem, and asked for consideration. The attendant said she would let it pass and didn't charge her extra.

Right behind Janet were two women whose luggage was also oversize. When the attendant told them, one of the women cursed the attendant and told her no one had ever told her that before and she wasn't about to pay extra. I think you know what happened. The attendant told her she didn't have to pay, but her luggage would not go on that flight that day.

The lady cursed again, took out her credit card, and paid the extra $25 for her luggage. The attendant left her station, went over and talked to two of her coworkers, and slowly took her time checking them in. They missed their flight.

You know what? Rude behavior is expensive!

## WHEN YOU'RE ON THE PLANE

Please put your hands over your mouth when you sneeze. The air on the plane doesn't circulate; thus, germs are easily spread. Shout-out to Airborne!

No loud talking. Some of us are trying to sleep.

Bring lots of books, toys, and other distractions for your children. Kids get antsy and need something to keep them entertained or occupied.

Some of y'all are scared to get on the plane, so none of this applies to you.

ADVANCE YOUR SWAGGER

# CONFIDENCE

ADVANCE YOUR SWAGGER

WHATEVER YOU DO, STRIVE TO

DO IT SO WELL THAT NO MAN

LIVING AND NO MAN DEAD,

AND NO MAN YET TO BE BORN

CAN DO IT ANY BETTER.

—DR. BENJAMIN ELIJAH MAYS

ADVANCE YOUR SWAGGER

ADVANCE YOUR SWAGGER

ADVANCE YOUR SWAGGER

ADVANCE YOUR SWAGGER

# CHAPTER 9

# BODY LANGUAGE

Remember how, in Chapter 1, I told you that I got the job with Diddy when I looked him straight in the eyes and told him I wouldn't take no for an answer? Deep down inside, I was scared to death. After all, I knew that I couldn't continue at the restaurant; yet I still had rent to pay and very little money. I had no other choice but to go full throttle. I had to draw on every lesson I'd ever learned, because I was confident I was the right man for the job at the right time. My body language played an important role in helping Diddy realize that, too.

So let's go over a few tips about body language and see the role it plays in helping you build your confidence.

## THE EYES HAVE IT

This guy seems interesting. I think I'd like to hear more.

BENT HINT: Looking people in the eyes says you have nothing to hide. It says you're confident in who you are and what you're saying. It adds a touch of class to your whole body language. Trust me on this. I have a lot of people tell me they are uncomfortable looking people in the eyes. If this doesn't feel right for you, practice it on a friend. I've learned if you look at the top part of a person's nose, it gives the impression that you're looking him or her in the eyes. Try it.

## GET THE HANDSHAKE RIGHT

Your handshake can say so much about you. It should be firm, and be sure to clasp the entire hand of the other person.

### Do

>Formal handshake: You should always shake hands as if you are the CEO of a Fortune 500 company.

Take the entire hand for a confident handshake.

A wimpy handshake makes you seem like a wimp. Women want the same handshake as everyone else. Leave her fingertips alone!

### Don'ts

Wimpy handshake: I call this the dead fish. It is completely undesirable.

Just-the-fingers handshake: Some gentlemen do this to ladies, thinking they might hurt a woman's hand, but I can tell you, it drives women nuts.

You're-killing-me handshake: For those of you with Napoleon complexes, or if you've begun lifting weights and you see a little difference in your biceps, please don't bring people to their knees with your handshake. For the ladies, you have nothing to prove by giving a too-firm handshake.

Homeboy handshake: This is for your homies only. Don't try to do something you saw somebody else doing; you may do it in the wrong neighborhood.

Clammy/wet handshake: Keep some paper towels. I got to keep it real. I don't know what to say about this one—go see your doctor.

## I LIKE THE WAY YOU MOVE

I know you've heard the saying "You never get a second chance to make a first impression." That's so true. You have only five seconds to make a good, bad, or ugly impression on people.

When you walk in a room, how are you looking? Does your dress, your swagger, your attitude say "I am here and I belong here"? Or does your dress and attitude say "I know I don't belong, but please let me in"? In other words, when you walk into the room, you have to act like you *own the room*.

The "bro" handshake is just for your homies. Don't take it to the office.

## IT REALLY IS OKAY TO SMILE

Whenever I see a hip-hop magazine, everyone in it appears angry. What's up with that? I bet when they got that call saying they had a contract, they were smiling. So why the long face? Half of y'all don't look so tough, anyway.

## YOUR BODY READS LIKE A BOOK

Keep in mind, your body is talking even when your mouth is closed. Paying close attention to your body language can help you enhance your confidence.

Kareem owns this joint—let him in!

This is the same guy, but look how his body language has changed. Lock the door!

Yeah, right, you don't believe what you're saying, and neither do I.

You talk too much, and I'm bored.

Okay, I get it!

The CEO
stance. I don't
know why they
like this pose,
but they do.

You're too close,
man. Back off!

# CHAPTER 10

# MAKING INTRODUCTIONS

## MEET MY FRIEND

I don't know about you, but introducing people always hangs me up. I always forget whose name to say first. When people tell me to introduce the oldest person to the youngest person, I never know if they mean to say the oldest person's name first or the youngest person's name first. That's why I try to keep it simple. Here are a few examples that work for me.

### Introduction #1

My ninety-year-old grandmother Nana is in town, and I want to introduce her to my neighbor.

Nana, this is one of my neighbors, Shannon. Shannon, please meet my grandmother Nana, who is visiting me from Columbus, Georgia.

*Watch this:* I said my grandmother's name first because she has the highest ranking over my neighbor or anyone I would introduce her to. Make sense?

## Introduction #2

I want to introduce my brother, Dion, to John Brown, a high-ranking executive in the industry.

John, I would like to introduce you to my brother, Dion. Dion is a graduate student at the University of Southern California. Dion, this is John Brown, senior vice president of Hancock Records.

*Watch this:* I said John's name first because he is the highest-ranking person in this introduction. I told John a little about Dion and told Dion a little about John. That will help give a jumping-off place to begin a conversation.

## Introduction #3

I want to introduce my friend Marcia to another friend, Dave. Both are in the same age group.

Marcia, this is my homeboy Dave. Dave graduated from Morehouse with me. Dave, meet Marcia. Marcia and I have been friends since sixth grade.

*Watch this:* I didn't use last names. That's okay if two people are from the same age group. Notice I said Marcia's name first because she is female. Our generation is not too concerned about this, but I'm still the southern gentleman, and I try to practice old-fashioned values like "ladies first." I don't always follow this rule, but it's good to know the rule and then decide if you want to break it.

## Introduction #4

I am with a very good friend, Chico. Another guy I know walks up, but I can't think of his name for the life of me. What to do?

Hey, man, what's going on? You know my friend, Chico, don't you? [Then you pray the other person will say his name.] If he doesn't, you pray Chico will say something like "Yes, I think we've met. What's your name again?"

*Watch this:* Because I'm terrible with names and I meet a lot of people, I've told all my friends if I don't say a person's name when he or she first comes up, I need them to go ahead and introduce themselves. Trust me, this has gotten me out of a lot of jams.

BENT HINT: Don't sweat over any of this introduction stuff. The main thing is not to leave people hanging. If you're talking to a friend and someone else walks up, use your own creativity to connect the two people. Whose name is said first is not nearly as important as helping people make the connection and not leaving anyone out.

# CHAPTER 11

# HELP ME LAND THAT JOB!

L
et me tell you what a typical day in my life is like. When I go to the mall or out to dinner, dreamers are going to seek me out. Dreamers who are just like I was. They, too, want to break into the entertainment business, or want to be a personal assistant, or simply want a job. I'm sure most of these people are really talented and might have what it takes to be successful. The unfortunate thing is many don't know how to get to first base with me or with anyone in the business because they don't know how to approach someone or market their work.

Some will interrupt me while I'm talking to someone else; others will shove a CD in my hand and keep moving, never stopping long enough to introduce themselves; and some will hand me their résumé or CD with no business card or contact information anywhere to be found. Even if I like their work, I won't know how to get in touch with them. If you do that much work to create a CD or write a résumé, have enough respect for yourself and your work to put a decent cover on it.

Here are a few tips that I think can help you land that position so you can get your check.

## DO YOUR HOMEWORK

Don't go for a job interview without doing your homework. Before I texted Diddy to ask him for a job, I researched him. I knew a lot about his background, his business ventures, and his demanding schedule. (I have to admit, I didn't know just how demanding it was. He is definitely the hardest-working man in the industry.) Having this knowledge about him helped me land the job.

Before you run off for that job interview, get on the Internet and research the company or person. Try to find out as much as you can about the product, services, customers, competitors, and work environment. Go to the office and walk around if you can. See how the people who work there dress. Is it strictly business? Is it a laid-back, very casual workplace? What you learn will help you know what to wear for your job interview.

Okay, you're in. You got the interview. Now what?

## GO ALONE

My first job after graduating from college was working in a retail store. The day I went to the store to apply, I went alone. A few minutes later, I looked up, and three guys and two girls walked in together and asked for applications. The manager immediately told them they didn't have any openings. They turned around and walked away. The manager turned to me, gave me an application, interviewed me, and offered me the job.

## BE ON TIME!

There's never an excuse good enough for being late for a job interview. You must get there on time. Better yet, you should get there at least ten minutes before your interview begins. This will give you time to catch your breath, survey the environment, and let people know you are about business. Try not to get there too early (twenty minutes or more), because they won't be ready for you and might be annoyed with you for interrupting their time. If you get to the appointment too early, don't go in. Stay outside, drive around, or do something until no more than ten minutes before your interview.

## A SMILE CAN MAKE YOUR DAY

Your interview starts the minute you walk in the door. A smile always sets the tone for a good day.

## THE EYES HAVE IT

Remember to look the person in the eyes (see the Bent Hint on p. 54). By the way, please don't wear shades into a job interview.

## WAIT!

When you enter the interviewer's office, don't sit down until you have been offered a seat. You can't just walk into someone's office and make yourself at home. Wait until he or she asks you to sit down. If the interviewer forgets to offer, then it's okay for you to ask, "Shall I sit here?" or "Where would you like for me to sit?" Then take your seat.

## KEEP YOUR STUFF OFF THE DESK

Don't put your personal stuff on the interviewer's desk. You should bring along only a folder with your résumé, a notepad, your business cards, and a pen. These things should stay on your lap and not on someone else's desk.

## TELL ME ABOUT YOURSELF

An interviewer doesn't want to know what hospital you were born in or who your first-grade teacher was. This is a way of checking out how well you can say a lot in a short amount of time. Be prepared to say three significant things about yourself, such as where you're from, where you went to school, and what your work experience is like. Make it short, simple, and to the point. Stay focused.

## MAKE LEMONADE OUT OF LEMONS

If your last job was the job from hell, don't complain about it. You can share that the work was not as challenging as you would have liked, or the company is transitioning and you need to explore other options. Don't blast your former employer or former boss. I made a major mistake once by sharing a work experience that I thought was off the record only to read about it in a major magazine. And even though it wasn't a job interview, it wasn't cool to talk negatively about an old work situation. Lesson learned. I will never do that again. Keep your interview positive, and positive things will come back to you.

## WHAT'S YOUR QUESTION?

Always have one or two good questions to ask the interviewer. This says you have done your homework and you are interested in learning more about the company. Do not ask about the salary or about benefits. There is plenty of time to get those questions answered. The focus of your questions should be on the company. What are the company's long-term and short-term goals? What's the vision of the CEO? What are the core values of the company? What are the written and unwritten values?

## CLOSE THE DEAL

Once the interview is over and you know this is the job you want, don't get out of your chair until you ask for it. In sales, it's called closing the deal. I've talked to a lot of people in hiring positions, and they've told me many people didn't get the job because they didn't ask for it. Remember, I told Diddy I couldn't take no for an answer. I made it very clear to him that I really wanted the job and would be the best personal assistant he'd ever seen. If you want it, ask for it!

## THANK-YOU NOTE

This is a little tip that few people use. When the interview is over, send a thank-you note via U.S. mail no later than the next day. Do not send it via e-mail. It won't mean as much. The handwritten note should thank the interviewer for taking the time to interview you. Let him or her know how much you enjoyed learning more about the company, and say that you know you will add value to the team. A little goes a long way. Even if you don't get that particular job, sending the note might help keep you on the radar screen for future opportunities. I told you, "thank you" is magical.

Got it? Now go get your check!

# CHAPTER 12

# MOVING ON UP

## DO MORE IF YOU WANT MORE

I started my career in the entertainment business as Diddy's personal assistant, but I wanted more. So I had to do more. I got to work early and
left late, very late. After working in my position for several months and
dazzling my boss with my performance, I made it a point to "lend" myself
to executives in other departments within the Bad Boy organization. This
gave me an opportunity to learn the totality of Diddy's businesses and,
many times, demonstrate my talents to his executives in their respective
genres.

BENT HINT: Be careful how you work this. You have to make sure you
are doing the best possible job in your present position before you try
to step outside of it. There is an old saying: "Blossom where you are
planted." If you're not careful, you can lose the job you have while
you're aiming for the next job. Stay focused.

## THINK AHEAD

Diddy loved a particular type of sunglasses. I noticed that out of all his shades, he always picked this particular brand to wear. After he lost his favorite pair once, I thought ahead and ordered forty pairs from the company. It's a good thing I did, because that particular style was discontinued.

## BE FLEXIBLE

When you start a new job, you need to be flexible as often as possible. There might be times when you need to give up some of your personal time to accommodate the needs of the organization. I missed out on a lot of dates with my girl during this time.

## UNDERPROMISE AND OVERDELIVER

I have learned that it's best to say you can't do something and do it than to say you can do something and don't. Or to say you need five days to complete a project and complete it in three days vs. saying you can complete a project in three days and do it in five days. In other words, it's best to underpromise and overdeliver than overpromise and underdeliver. Got it?

## NETWORK, NETWORK, NETWORK

Don't expect to get the big hookup the first time you meet someone. I have so many people come up to me and say, "Hey, Bent, will you give this CD to Kanye?" Are you kidding me? Who are you? It's all about timing and establishing a rapport.

BENT HINT: I had seen Diddy around town and had known him for almost five years before I reached out to him and asked for an opportunity.

## IF YOU'RE WORTH IT, ASK FOR IT

No one can read your mind. If you want a promotion or a raise, you'd better ask somebody. Make sure you clearly communicate your accomplishments, your value to the organization, and why you merit the next position or raise. If you don't toot your own horn, nobody else will. Speaking of tooting, make sure you're in tune. This is a "tongue in cheek" comment by Deull—tooting your *horn*—make sure it's in tune. Get it?

## IF THE JOB DOESN'T FIT, YOU MUST A'QUIT

If the job is not right for you, it's not good for you or the organization for you to hang on. Treat it like a new pair of shoes—if they don't fit, give 'em back. Your employer will appreciate your honesty, and you will be able to sleep at night. But make sure you have something on deck, otherwise you are now unemployed. It's easier to get a job when you already have one.

BENT HINT: Don't burn any bridges. Always leave a job in a positive way, just in case you need to go back. Plus, you will need your old boss for a reference.

# STYLE

ADVANCE YOUR SWAGGER

ADVANCE YOUR SWAGGER

I DON'T DESIGN CLOTHES,

I DESIGN DREAMS.

—RALPH LAUREN

ADVANCE YOUR SWAGGER

ADVANCE YOUR SWAGGER

ADVANCE YOUR SWAGGER

ADVANCE YOUR SWAGGER

ADVANCE YOUR SWAGGER

ADVANCE YOUR SWAGGER

# CHAPTER 13

# SO FRESH AND SO CLEAN, CLEAN

I can't begin talking about style until we discuss hygiene. You must get and keep your body fresh and clean before you put on that double-breasted blue blazer or that sexy red-hot miniskirt. It doesn't matter how good you look if you have bad body odor.

## WHAT'S THAT SMELL?

I was contracted to assist a very famous singer with his wardrobe. This musical genius was about the same height and size as me, so I took over a few of my personal clothes for him to try on. I wanted to get a sense of his style and taste. He tried on two of my favorite and most expensive shirts. I really hate to tell you this, but when he took them off, they were so funky that I had to throw them away. I didn't think the cleaners could get the stench out.

The sad part about this story is, this guy has lots of friends. Why is it that no one has told him the truth about his body odor? Most people, even your best friends and family, may have a hard time telling you the truth about your odor. The best way to ensure you don't have people talking behind your back is for you to keep your body clean at all times. If you have an ongoing issue with bad body odor, check it out with your doctor. You might need more than Irish Spring.

Give your body a complete cleaning every day. Twice a day if you work out or sweat a lot. When I was in college, we used to take what we called a "sign of the cross" sponge bath—you know, you hit only those "essential" parts. Not good enough. Get in the shower or tub. Your entire body is essential!

Remember to use deodorant. It's also a good idea to use lotion or Vaseline to make sure you don't show up ashy. Not a good look.

## SLOW HANDS AND HAPPY FEET

There is another detail that no one will tell you about but people notice. Men and women with dirty, unkempt nails are thought to be careless, unclean, and unprofessional. Therefore, both women and men need to do regular manicures and pedicures. You need to keep your nails clean and cuticles pushed back. You can buy your own nail file and do your nails yourself, get a friend to do it for you, or go to a professional nail salon. What works for your fingernails is also needed for your toenails, especially in the summer, if you're wearing sandals. Take the time to take care of those nails. It really does matter. Go treat yourself to a wonderful and relaxing manicure/pedicure. Fellas, don't hate on it if you haven't tried it.

Ah, man, I'm relaxed. Brothers, if you haven't tried a manicure or pedicure, don't hate on it!

Every woman deserves to be treated like a queen.

## YOUR CROWNING GLORY

Your hair needs a good shampooing at least once a week and a good deep conditioner at least once a month. I am reminded of the movie *It's a Wonderful Life*. Remember the scene with Jimmy Stewart smelling Donna Reed's hair while they were talking on the phone? It was the fresh smell of her hair that clinched the ring!

I've seen all kinds of hairstyles out there. Listen up, ladies. If you wear a weave, make sure your tracks don't show. If you wear a wig, make sure it won't blow off.

I was at church recently when a baby began to cry. The mother got up to take her baby out, and as they were walking out of the church, the entire congregation began to laugh. The baby had picked up the wig of a lady sitting next to the aisle. The lady ran behind the mother and the baby, trying to get her wig back. I have to admit, I cracked up. I haven't seen that lady back at church since.

Tie down that wig!

## SAY CHEESE

Brushing your teeth is important—that is if you still want them when you get older. You should brush your teeth twice a day, in the morning and before you go to bed. And my dentist always reminds me to floss, which I hate to do. Speaking of the dentist, you really need to see your dentist twice a year for a thorough cleaning.

BENT HINT: If you brush your tongue and the roof of your mouth, it will help cut down on bad breath.

# CHAPTER 14

# THREADS AND VINES

When I was in the eighth grade, the latest and greatest fashion fad was pajama-like outfits called "skids." Skids shirts and pants were extremely colorful, and they came in stripes, flowers, or any design you could think of. Everyone had them. I had to have every design they made. I told my parents all I wanted for Christmas were skids. My dad tried to talk me out of it, but I prevailed. My parents gave me $500 for Christmas, and I went shopping. I bought every pair of skids they had in my size. I was the happiest kid on my street that Christmas.

Then spring came.

By spring, skids were completely out of style. You looked like a fool in those crazy parachute-like pants with all of those crazy colors. I had spent all of my Christmas money on those outfits, and three months later, they were out of style. Man!

That was when my lesson in fashion began.

My dad bought me a book, *Clothes and the Man: The Principles of Fine Men's Dress* by Alan Flusser. He sat me down and talked to me about timeless, quality fashion. He took me to the Polo store and showed me blazers, pants, and shirts that had been in style for ten, twenty, thirty years or more and were still in style today. I was blown away.

I began my own research and understanding of style. From that point on, I made a decision to buy only classic, timeless clothes. Anything other than that was a waste of time and money. Of course, I learned how to put my own twist on the classics, but classic was the way to go for me. My friends started calling me "Poloman."

As fate had it, when I moved to New York, I had a chance to meet and apprentice with Alan Flusser. It was Alan who encouraged me to attend Fashion Institute of Technology (FIT) to learn about textiles and how to get the right drape and silhouette. The class was priceless.

## WHAT SHOULD I WEAR?

Before you walk out of your house to go anyplace, you need to ask yourself, "What should I wear?" The answer depends on three other questions:

Where am I going?

What do I want to communicate about myself?

What is the appropriate attire for the occasion?

What to wear depends on how you answer these questions. What you wear at the beach is a totally different look from what you wear to church. What you wear for a job interview is totally different from what you wear to a club.

I've seen a lot of people get it twisted. I've seen some of y'all in the office wearing something that you had on at the club. It's all about being appropriate for the occasion. Your dress, like your body language, communicates a lot about who you are and what you're selling.

## MEET ME IN THE MALL

### Don'ts

Take a look at these pictures of folks I actually met in the mall. Now, tell me, what are they selling? Keep it real. Check out the mirror before you walk out the door. You never know who's watching.

What are they selling?

# IT'S ABOUT THE FIT

A lot of guys think it makes them look hard to have their pants down below their butts. But if something were to go down and they had to run, it would be hard to get away running wide-legged. Think about that.

Brothers, pick up your pants. No one, and I mean no one, wants to look at your butt. It's not cool, and it can't be comfortable. Why walk around wide-legged when you don't have to? That's why the belt was invented, man! Buy one!

I know you can see that the hip-hop game is changing. The giants in the business are no longer wearing their pants below their butts, and most are not wearing those oversize shirts and suits. They are striving to be elegantly appointed.

The first thing I did when I started working for Diddy was take all of his suits to a tailor and have them sized to fit him. At the time he wore his clothes too big. It was important for him to represent, to set the standard, and to be the role model for the entire hip-hop community. After all, if I was going to be his personal assistant, he had to get it right. That was my job!

82

He loved his new look, and it became his inspiration for designing his new Sean John line. He later went on to win the prestigious Council of Fashion Designers of America (CFDA) Award, the most notable award you can get in the fashion industry.

Gentlemen: Find a good tailor. He can make all the difference. Right now I can get a basic suit from Banana Republic and take it to my tailor, and I will look better than someone who buys a Brioni and doesn't use a tailor.

## SIZING YOUR PANTS

Your pants waist belongs on your natural waist. That's it! I have nothing else to say about that.

The length of your pants should fall at the top of your shoe, and the back of your pants should slant toward the heel of your shoe. When you walk, your socks should not be seen. When you sit, your leg should not show.

This is my friend Jay Kos, who is the designer and owner of Jay Kos clothing store in New York. His swagger is legendary. Here he shows us where the waist of a man's pants should be.

Brother, please pick up those pants!

## SIZING YOUR SHIRT

Every man, no matter how young or how old, should know the size of his neck and arm. If you don't know, you can go to your nearest department store and ask someone in the men's suit department to measure you. Don't buy a shirt until you get this sizing done. I have seen too many men in very expensive suits, but they looked cheap because the neck of their shirt was either too little or way too big. Either way, it's not a good look. Get sized. It's free.

Ladies: The right fit is very important for you, too! Before you buy that size six, make sure you can wear it without showing the bulges. That's not a good look. I don't think the size is nearly as important as the fit. Check it out. You'll thank me one day.

Men, getting your shirts and jackets sized is a good look. Here's Nino sizing Rapper Chase Phoenix's shirt and Jay's jacket.

BENT HINT: Buying expensive clothes is not necessary to get a good look. Buying clothes that fit properly is. Take the time to get measured, and buy your clothes accordingly.

For both men and women, a good tailor can make all the difference. It's amazing how the right fit can transform an item of clothing. This is Nino, the tailor.

Clothes should be an investment. I think it's better to have a few time-less pieces than to have a bunch of trendy pieces that will go out of style before the end of the season. Remember the skids?

Here are some ways to walk out the door and be on top of your game, no matter where you're going.

### Fifteen Things Every Man Should Have in His Closet

1. A navy blazer: This is a classic look that works with jeans. And it looks great with gray, cream, white, or just about any color pants. You can dress it up or dress it down. It's a must.

2. A corduroy sport jacket: This timeless jacket also works with most pants. It's different, yet it's been around forever, and it makes you look fantastic.

3. Suits: You must have a navy suit and a gray suit. They work for job interviews, church, weddings, and just about anywhere.

BENT HINT: If you see a three-piece suit, get it. Each piece can be worn with other things.

4. Pants: Cream gabardine and gray flannel. Invest in these two pairs of pants, and they will go with you anywhere for many years to come, or until your gut bursts out of them.

5. Shirts: White and blue dress shirts are a must. You should also have a check, a stripe, and a colored shirt, such as lavender or pink. I recommend that every man have a formal white shirt in his closet. You can rent the tux, but buy your own shirt.

6. Cargo pants: These are also timeless pants. They can be dressed up or dressed down and look great.

7. Jeans: You know you gotta have these, and make sure you get the right fit. I personally prefer Earnest Sewn jeans.

8. Sweaters: A black or navy turtleneck works for casual, business, and formal occasions. For spring/summer, a lightweight V-neck is always a great addition to your wardrobe.

9. Footwear: Invest in a good pair of brown suedes and a pair of black or chestnut bench-made shoes. They will go with any suit.

10. Socks or men's hosiery: Use this accessory to add your own flavor to your ensemble. You can go with classic black or brown, or put a little color on your feet. I prefer over-the-calf socks to make sure your legs don't show when you sit.

11. Ties: Seven-fold ties are always the best, but you can find great ties just about anywhere. I recommend you get to know a sales associate in a boutique or department store and tell him or her to call you when a new shipment of ties comes in, as well as when they go on sale.

12. Belts/suspenders/braces: Belts can be expensive. Again, see the expense as an investment, so go ahead and buy that alligator or croc belt. They look good and will last forever. Keep in mind, suspenders clamp on to your trousers, and braces button into trousers. I prefer braces.

BENT HINT: Please don't wear a belt and suspenders or braces at the same time. They do the same thing, and it's just incorrect.

13. Pocket squares: If you wear a suit or jacket with a front pocket, you are not completely dressed without a pocket square. You can never have enough pocket squares. You usually see them in cotton or silk, but if you see a nice cashmere one, go for it: It will look great in your corduroy jacket.

14. An umbrella: Don't leave home without it. It adds a touch of elegance, completes your ensemble, helps protect you from the elements, and can get you extra points with the ladies.

15. Hats: I need to devote a complete section to this, because I happen to be a lover of hats. I think men in America stopped the tradition of wearing hats when John F. Kennedy became the first president of the United States who didn't wear one at his inauguration. Too bad.

My great-grandfather Daddy Emmitt was my inspiration for being elegantly appointed. When Daddy Emmitt walked out of the house, you'd better believe a fedora was on his head. As a child, I used to admire the pride he took in his dress. Daddy Emmitt used to always say, "A man who doesn't care about how he looks doesn't care about much." He was married to Mama Gail for seventy years and left a legacy of style and commitment to family that was carried on by my grandfather Oscar and my dad Fred. I had to get it right!

My rule of thumb for men wearing a hat is simple: When you're indoors, take it off. Brothers, even when your hat matches that bad outfit you just bought, take it off when you're indoors! When you're outdoors, put it on. You should always remove your hat when the national anthem is being played, when the U.S. flag is passing by, or when you're at a grave site.

Fast-food restaurants and a few casual dining restaurants don't mind if men keep a cap on while they're eating. But if it's a white-tablecloth restaurant, all hats have to go!

Ladies, you can wear hats just about any time, except in the office and with formal wear.

## THE STYLE OF A WOMAN

For this section on women's attire, I reached out to my friend Sari Tertelbaum, store manager for Zari Boutique in New York. Sari helped me formulate what every woman must have in her closet.

**Fifteen Things Every Woman Should Have in Her Closet**

1. A black pantsuit: You can dress it up or dress it down. It can be paired with all colors and any type of blouse, shirt, sweater, or a simple long strand of pearls. The best part is you can split it up. You can wear the pants with another top, or wear the jacket with other pants or a skirt. If you don't have this wonder in your closet, put down this book and run to the mall and buy one.

2. A little black dress: Audrey Hepburn made this dress popular back in the day, and it's still popular today. Again, it goes with everything; this dress can be worn anywhere, and you will look like a million bucks.

3. A classic white button-down shirt: This looks fantastic with jeans, with that pantsuit, or with black leggings and a belt.

4. Jeans: You already know. No closet can be complete without the right pair of jeans that make your butt look good. Be sure to take your best and most honest friend with you to help make sure you get the right fit. Jeans paired with the right shoes look good in the park or at a concert.

5. A cardigan sweater, any color: You can throw this over your shoulders and be good to go. Jackie Kennedy made this look classic. It adds a touch of class to whatever you have on.

6. A big bag: A bag that can carry everything is important. It's good to have a small bag inside the big bag so that if you want to stop by a happy hour after work, you can take out your small one and be good to go.

7. A trench coat: This is a coat for almost all seasons. It goes with everything and is appropriate for just about any occasion.

8. A jogging suit: An attractive jogging suit (preferably velour) is perfect for that trip to the market, for a quick lunch with friends, and for a manicure and pedicure at the spa. It's comfortable and looks great on.

9. Jewelry: A long strand of white pearls is a must. Again, you can thank Audrey for this. The best part is you can't tell the real from the fake. Nobody cares, anyway. You also need a great pair of stud earrings (could be pearls, gold, or silver) and a wonderful pair of large hoop earrings.

10. Bangles, bangles, bangles: Go raid your mother's jewelry case. Get her bangles from the sixties and seventies. Mix them up. They look great!

11. Footwear: I know it's hard for a woman to get away with just one pair of shoes. I think you should have a high-heeled black pump, brown and/or beige sling backs, and why not, a pair of reds. Make sure you have a pair of pointed-toe heels and a pair of round-toe heels. You should also splurge and get a pair of black or brown boots with a detail like a buckle or a chain. The boots can be your fashion statement or your weapon if you need to kick some guy who's gotten out

of hand. You need to have sneakers and a pair of bejeweled flat sandals as well as a pair of bejeweled high-heeled sandals.

12. Hosiery: A pair of black leggings. They look good with your white shirt, your little black dress, and just about everything.

13. A hat: You need a hat for those bad-hair days. Be sure to try it on and get the right fit for your face.

14. A belt: A wide belt in black or red works with almost anything.

15. An umbrella: Don't leave home without it. This is a perfect fashion statement that can enhance your look and add that element of protection. Make sure it's a Bentley Signature one . . . HOLLA!

# CHAPTER 16

# THE THREE HOW-TOS

There are two very basic things that I think all men should know how to do but for some reason don't: tie a necktie and tie a bow tie. When I asked my cousin Marcia what was the one thing she thought all women should do but can't do well, she said, "Put on makeup."

With that in mind, I am dedicating this section of the book to these three things.

## HOW TO TIE A NECKTIE

Here's the deal: If you don't know how to tie a tie, you are not a Grown-A— Man. Every man should know how to tie a tie, even if he only wears it to weddings and funerals. I ain't mad at you, but come on, dog, get this one right.

There are two sides to a tie—a wide side and a narrow side.

Cross the wide side over the narrow side.

Pull the wide side under the narrow side and back through the loop. The wide side should be inside out.

Bring the wide side down and through the knot in front.

Use both hands to tighten the knot and carefully draw the knot up to the collar.

Bing-a-bang. The Windsor knot!

## HOW TO TIE A BOW TIE

I'm amazed when I see our superstars going to the Oscars with a clip-on tie. What's up with that? These men need to learn how to tie a bow tie or at least make sure their stylist or personal assistant knows how.

Place the bow tie around your neck so that one end is about two inches longer than the other.

Cross the longer side over the shorter side.

Bring the longer side up and under to form a loop. Pull the loop tight.

Take both hands and pull one end down.

Now double that end under itself.

Double the other end back on itself and place it through the loop behind the bow tie.

Adjust the bow tie by pulling at the end and straightening the center knot.

There you have it!

## ALL MADE UP

Ladies, please pay attention to this: Makeup is a good thing, but too much of anything is too much. I'm sure every man has an opinion about how much or how little makeup he likes to see on his lady. As for me, I think a little is more. I like the natural-beauty look. I believe makeup should enhance your look, not change it altogether. I want to know it's still you behind all that powder and lipstick.

Here's Marcia demonstrating the step-by-step way to put on just enough makeup.

After cleaning your face and applying a sunscreen, it may be necessary to use a concealer to cover dark circles under the eyes and/or any discoloration.

Apply your foundation with a sponge to even out your skin tone.

Dust on a light layer of loose powder for a softer more natural look.

Apply a light coat of mascara to enhance the eyelashes. One or two coats should do the job.

Put your smile on and add the blush to the apple of your cheeks—blend it in so it doesn't show a harsh line.

To get a more natural look use a lipstick brush to apply your lipstick. You might also choose to use a lip liner to outline your lips.

You now have a clean natural look and you're good to go.

And too much!

Be sure NOT to overdo your makeup. Remember, makeup is used to enhance your beauty, not create it.

# EPILOGUE: DEALING WITH HATERS

"Manservant." "Butler." These are just some of the names I've been called by people I don't know and who don't know me.

Keep in mind, the whole celebrity thing was new to me when I began working for Diddy. I didn't know how to handle any kind of press, and I most definitely didn't know how to handle this kind of mean-spirited negative press. It was a very painful and difficult period in my life. You can't begin to imagine how my parents, family, and friends felt when they read all those things about me. They knew me. They knew what my goal was and what I was trying to do to reach it. They knew how hard I was working. Yet they had to deal with all that negative stuff being said about me.

My mother called me in tears one day and begged me to leave, to move back to Atlanta, and to get a nice corporate job. Moms are moms, and they do what they do—worry! I love my mother and thank God for her every day, but I couldn't do what she was asking me to do. My dad had a different take on the situation. He reminded me of an old African proverb: "It doesn't matter what you are called but what you answer to."

That was it! Those were the words I needed to hear, and they came at the right time. I had to get my eyes back on the prize.

This whole episode reminded me of my track days back in high school and in college. I ran the 400, 800, and 1600 meters. I could hear the voices of Coach Aftel at North Atlanta High School and Coach Hill at Morehouse College ringing in my ears: "Run your race, stay in your lane, and do your personal best!" Those words helped me get through every race I ran on the track, and they helped me get through that college, a crazy period in my life.

Think about it—in life, there are always people on the sidelines. Some are there to cheer you on, and others are there to boo you in hopes that they can throw you off course. If you want to win, you must keep your eyes on your prize. You must run your race, stay in your lane, and give your personal best no matter what. Haters usually show up when you're doing something they want to do but can't, or you're doing something they don't want to see you do because you might get ahead of them. Guess what? That's their problem, not yours.

While people were hating on me, I was traveling to Chile with Cameron Diaz and Drew Barrymore . . . ah, two Charlie's Angels! While people were hating on me, I was interviewing people like Will Smith, James Brown, Robert De Niro, Martin Scorsese, and Jamie Foxx for *Access Hollywood*. While people were hating on me, I was in the studio with Kanye West, André 3000, and Big Boi. See what I mean? I didn't have a problem. The haters did. I kept my eyes on my prize.

Let me warn you, the same will happen to you. Once you get your swagger on, and you begin using the manners of our elders, and you begin to feel confident in yourself and your talent, and your style becomes your personal brand, get ready. The haters are coming! The haters are coming! They don't want to see you get ahead. They don't want to see you move from a powerless position to a powerful position. After all, who do you think you are?

Your homies might call you names that you sho 'nuff don't want your mama to hear. They might get mad at you because of your new behavior and your new look. They don't understand why you're going through these changes, and they don't like it. Don't let that stop you. In the words of that famous prophet Katt Williams, "If you got twelve people hating on you, figure out how to make it fourteen. You must be doing something right."

Keep moving. Keep growing. Stay focused.

You now know there's another way to live. It's not necessarily better or worse; it's all about choice. You can choose what works best for you. When you didn't know what you didn't know, you had to do the best you could. Now you have options.

You now know:

1. Manners matter: Don't forget those little things that help define how you treat people and how people treat you.
2. Confidence matters: If you don't believe in yourself, why should anybody else?
3. Style matters: Taking care of your body and what you wrap it in might just help you increase your value.

I hope this book has given you some of the basics that will help you advance your swagger. I hope you have learned enough to make you want to learn more and do more. Once you've learned, you must share it with others. As my maternal great-grandfather used to say, "Learn, then teach." I'm still learning. How about you?

I'm ending this book the way I began: with my family. As you can see, "Since I was 9," I've had swagger. Now you know why! Pictured from left, clockwise: my mother, Harriette; my dad, Fred; me; and my brother, Dion.

And the tradition continues . . .

# WHAT'S YOUR SQ?

We all know about an IQ (Intelligence Quotient) test and perhaps you've heard about an EQ (Emotional Quotient) test, but I want to introduce you to "The SQ (Swagger Quotient)" test. Now, don't get intimidated. This is just a little somethin' somethin' to see how much you've learned and what you might need to go back and brush up on.

## ARE YOU READY? HERE GOES:

1. Your butter plate is always to the right of your plate.
   True        False

2. Your water glass is always to the left of your plate.
   True        False

3. You should begin eating when everyone at your table has been served.
   True        False

4. You should butter your entire roll before you eat it.

   True          False

5. You should never put your elbows on the table while eating.

   True          False

6. It's okay for a man to throw his tie over his shoulder when he eats.

   True          False

7. If you invite someone to lunch you are expected to pay.

   True          False

8. If you find hair in your food, you should let everyone in the restaurant know so they will be careful about what they're eating.

   True          False

9. When you're invited for dinner, you should order anything that's on the menu regardless of the price.

   True          False

10. If you put something in your mouth and you don't like it, you should discreetly remove it with your fork.

    True          False

11. If someone asks you to pass the salt shaker, you should pass the pepper shaker with it.

    True          False

12. You need to make reservations before you go to a fine-dining restaurant for dinner.

    True          False

13. Dutch treat means you will pay for the meal.

    True          False

14. When you place your fork and knife at the 3:15 position, it means you have finished eating and the waiter can take your plate.
    True        False

15. When you send a text message in all caps it means it's very important.
    True        False

16. If someone sends you a heated e-mail, you need to immediately respond to it with an e-mail.
    True        False

17. When you're invited to someone's house for dinner, you should bring a small gift.
    True        False

18. If you're invited to a party and one of your homies is in town, it's okay to take him/her with you.
    True        False

19. It's okay to take your drink into a store if you aren't finished with it.
    True        False

20. If an elderly person or pregnant woman gets on the bus, you should offer them your seat.
    True        False

21. It's okay to talk on the phone in the movie as long as you keep it low.
    True        False

22. In American culture, it's impolite to look people in the eyes.
    True        False

23. Men should only shake the fingers of a woman to make sure he doesn't hurt her hand.
    True        False

24. When you introduce an older person to a younger person, you should say the older person's name first.
    True        False

25. When you go for a job interview, it's best to take a friend with you.
    True        False

26. When you walk into an interviewer's office, it's good to put your briefcase on his/her table to demonstrate your confidence.
    True        False

27. It's okay to be late for a job interview if you call and give them a good excuse.
    True        False

28. During the interview the first thing you need to get straight is how much you will get paid.
    True        False

29. You should not talk badly about the boss you used to work for when you apply for a new job.
    True        False

30. When you complete your interview, you should get up, shake hands, and leave.
    True        False

31. If you get a job, you should make sure your boss knows you really want a better job than what you have.
    True        False

32. A man does not need a manicure.

    True    False

33. If you brush your tongue or the roof of your mouth, it can help cut down on bad breath.

    True    False

34. A man's pants should fall right below his beltline.

    True    False

35. Mens' necks don't grow that much, so they only need to get measured for a shirt every 15 to 20 years.

    True    False

36. A man can wear a hat indoors as long as it matches his suit.

    True    False

37. A woman should remove her hat when the national anthem is being played.

    True    False

38. If you want to be cool, you should go out and buy the hottest and most trendy clothes the minute they hit the stores.

    True    False

39. A blue blazer is timeless and will go with just about any pair of pants.

    True    False

40. The most important thing about clothes is that they must be expensive if you want to look good.

    True    False

## Answers

| | | | |
|---|---|---|---|
| 1.) F | 11.) T | 21.) F | 31.) F |
| 2.) F | 12.) T | 22.) F | 32.) F |
| 3.) T | 13.) F | 23.) F | 33.) T |
| 4.) F | 14.) T | 24.) T | 34.) F |
| 5.) T | 15.) F | 25.) F | 35.) F |
| 6.) F | 16.) F | 26.) F | 36.) F |
| 7.) T | 17.) T | 27.) F | 37.) F |
| 8.) F | 18.) F | 28.) F | 38.) F |
| 9.) F | 19.) F | 29.) T | 39.) T |
| 10.) T | 20.) T | 30.) F | 40.) F |

Key: If you got the following numbers correct:

| | |
|---|---|
| 37–40 | Your Swagger is on point |
| 31–36 | Your Swagger is a'ight |
| 25–30 | Your Swagger is suspect |
| Below 25 | What's a Swagger? |

# ACKNOWLEDGMENTS

This book would not have happened without my uncompromising belief in, and my dad's constant reminder of, Philippians 4:13 that reads,

> "I can do all things through Christ who strengthens me."

I thank my Heavenly Father for His Word and for keeping His promises, and I thank my earthly father for always pointing me back to Him.

I also want to thank the following people for their inspiration, assistance, and guidance in helping me along the way:

Andre Harrell who had the vision for this book.

Sean "Diddy" Combs, who believed in me from the start and gave me an opportunity of a lifetime.

Rashida Harrington, the best photographer in the world. Rashida received her masters in photography from the Savannah School of Arts & Science (SCAD) in 2006. They taught you well.

Jay Kos, owner extraordinaire of the finest haberdashery in New York City. Thanks for being a good friend and loyal supporter for many, many years.

Sari Tertelbaum, your style comes from the inside out. Thank you for your friendship.

Alan Flusser, the man of style. You will always be my inspiration.

I want to give a special shout out to my models: actress Faune Chambers, you were my number one long before *White Chicks* and *Epic movies*; Marcia Dore, my beautiful and creative cousin; Kareem Lawrence, my friend who's comfortable in his own skin; Grace Dore, my adorable little cousin, who played her part with grace; Rapper Chase Phoenix, Nino the tailor, and my mall pals for being themselves.

Special thanks to my gifted cousin, Jarrett Kelley, for his flavor; Wendy Credle, Nina Shaw, and Loan Dang, my legal team; and Michael McGowen at Mark Shale, Lenox Square, Atlanta.

There are several friends who hold me down, keep me in check, and always have my back: Big Boi, André 3000, Kanye West, Cameron Diaz, wil.i.am, UGK, Dave Howard, Chico Bryson, Hilton Hollaway, Rodney O'Neal McKnight, Cassidy Podell, Ryan Maltese, Bo Young, Cabral Franklin, Dr. Mustafa Davis, Keith Spelmon, Casey West, Stephen Smartt, Charles Owens, Greg Milton, Jeanette Dilone, Jessica and Denise Robinson, Maryse Thomas, and Quincy Jones, III, thank you!

I am blessed to have many spiritual leaders who pray for me, advise me, and help keep me grounded: Bishop Clarence E. McClendon, Rev. Melvin Wilson, Rev. Calvin Butts, Rev. Walter L. Kimbrough, Rev. Rich and Jane Berry, The Smartt family (go Brooklyn), and of course, Auntie Lisa.

I want to thank my mentors and advisors who mentor me close up and personally and from afar: Dr. Bill Cosby; Danny Meyer a.k.a. Mr. Hospitality; Richard Corraine; Jason and Haley Binn of Niche Media; Russell Simmons; Coach Aftel; Coach Hill; Mrs. Natalie Colbert; Mrs. Early; Dr. J. K. Haynes; the late Dean Blocker; the late Ella Yates; the late Dr. Clark; my wonderful aunts, Lurlyne, Calgene, Martha, Fan, Flossie,

Cornelius, and the late Sarah Kelley; Alfred, Theotis, Janice, Ashley, Christopher and Jonathan Watkins; James, Willie, Dwight, Erica and Robert Debro; Jeffrey and Carlos Clark; Stephanie Williams; Fredrick and Eric Dore; Derek and Felicia Spratley; Jerri Lee; Ambassador Andrew Young; Shirley Franklin, the Mayor of Atlanta; and the entire city of Atlanta . . . ahhh I'm so thankful you are a part of my life.

Thank you Melody Guy, one of the most patient and talented senior editors, for giving me the opportunity to write this book, for having the faith that I had something to share with others, and for guiding me every step of the way. I also want to thank Danielle Durkin, associate editor, and the entire team at Villard and Ballantine who helped bring this book to life. You guys are simply the best!

Very special thanks to my brilliant brother, Dion. We have always made and will continue to make inspirational art together. And, to all of my family and friends who encouraged me, pushed me, and gave me the confidence to know that I really could write a book, thank you.

We did it, MOM!

## ABOUT THE AUTHOR

The First Gentleman of Hip Hop, FONZWORTH BENTLEY, born Derek Watkins, graduated from Atlanta's Morehouse College with a bachelor of science degree concentrating in biology, then attended New York's prestigious Fashion Institute of Technology. After becoming one of the most popular maître d's in New York City, he raised his profile as Sean "Diddy" Combs's personal assistant. He later became style and fashion correspondent for *Access Hollywood,* covering the Oscars, Golden Globes, and Grammys. He is the executive producer of an upcoming album with Kanye West featuring André 3000, Faith Evans, Esthero, and Pimp C., among others. Fonzworth Bentley lives in Los Angeles. For information about Fonzworth Bentley's tour, news, special events, and his Advance Your Swagger contest, visit him on line at www.fonzworthbentley.net and www.myspace.com/therealbentley.